3/09

Living on the Edge
ROCK CLIMBING

Shane McFee

press.
New York

Published in 2008 by The Rosen Publishing Group, Inc.
29 East 21st Street, New York, NY 10010

First Edition

Editor: Joanne Randolph
Book Design: Kate Laczynski
Photo Researcher: Jessica Gerweck

Photo Credits: Cover, p. 1 © www.istockphoto.com/Eric Foltz; p. 4 © www.istockphoto.com/Simon Krzic; p. 6 © Getty Images, Inc.; p. 8 © www.istockphoto.com/Mike Dabell; p. 10 © www.istockphoto.com/Beverley Vycital; p. 12 © www.istockphoto.com/Mark Rose; p. 14 © www.istockphoto.com/Paulo Resende; p. 16 © www.istockphoto.com/Valerie Loiseleux; p. 18 © www.istockphoto.com/Ales Novak; p. 20 © www.istockphoto.com/Dave Pullicino.

Library of Congress Cataloging-in-Publication Data

McFee, Shane.
   Rock climbing / Shane McFee. — 1st ed.
      p. cm. — (Living on the edge)
   Includes index.
   ISBN 978-1-4042-4220-3 (library binding)
   1. Rock climbing—Juvenile literature. I. Title.
   GV200.2.M39 2008
   796.522'3—dc22
                                              2007038765

Manufactured in the United States of America

CONTENTS

Start Climbing!

Have you ever wanted to climb up the face of a cliff? Does this sound **dangerous**? It is. It is also fun. Many people from all over the world go rock climbing. The dangers of rock climbing give people a **thrill**.

Rock climbing is a very hard sport. It can take years to become a great climber. Climbers need to learn special climbing **maneuvers**. They must also learn how to use special climbing **equipment**. A small mistake can be deadly. Do you want to learn more? This book will tell you about this **extreme sport**.

This climber is moving sideways along a small rock shelf. You can see that there is a rope fixed to the rock to help her climb.

Mountaineers

The first rock climbers were mountaineers. A mountaineer is an **explorer** who climbs mountains. Mountaineering was very important in the 1880s and the 1900s. Mountaineers tried to reach the tops of the world's tallest mountains. Mountaineers needed to rock climb to get to the mountain peaks, or tops. The early mountaineers used **hooks** and ropes to climb these dangerous cliffs. Mountaineering was much more dangerous than rock climbing is today.

Mountaineers began to practice rock climbing on shorter rock walls and cliffs in England, Italy, and Germany. Rock climbing soon became a well-liked sport.

Here mountaineers cross a gap in the rock and ice using a rope and a ladder in 1900. Since then, climbing has become safer.

What You Need

The most important piece of rock-climbing equipment is rope. Climbing ropes are very strong. Some ropes are made to lessen the force of a fall. Other ropes are fixed to the rocks using **anchors**. Climbers use metal clips called **carabiners**. These tools help climbers handle the ropes.

Every rock climber should wear a **harness**. The harness holds the weight of the climber's body and allows for movement of arms and legs. Ropes are fixed to the harness. Rock climbers also use cams. Cams are used as anchors that can be moved when needed.

This climber's belt has carabiners, anchors, and other important tools. Because they keep you safe, another name for anchors is protection.

Making the Grade

Rock climbing cliffs are called routes. Each route has a certain grade. The grade tells you how hard and dangerous the route is to climb. Different countries have different grading systems.

The system that most American rock climbers use is called the Yosemite Decimal System. The Yosemite Decimal System grades go from 5.0 to 5.15. This system also adds the letter *a*, *b*, *c*, or *d* at the end of the number. For example, a 5.11a route is a little easier to climb than a 5.11b. The hardest routes are 5.15d.

Mt. McKinley, also called Denali, is one of the world's hardest mountains to climb. More than 90 climbers have died trying to reach the top.

How Does It Work?

Once a climber has picked his or her route, it is time to start climbing. Climbers place their hands and feet on places in the rock called holds. They climb from hold to hold. Climbers have to be very strong.

Most rock climbers climb in groups of two. There is usually one climber, or leader, and one belayer. The leader usually climbs ahead of the belayer. The belayer passes rope to the leader. This is called feeding the rope, or belaying.

The top of the route is called the pitch. When the leader reaches the pitch, he or she anchors the rope. It is now the belayer's turn to climb.

Here a climber works her way from hold to hold on her way up the rock. You can see the belayer on the ground.

How Do You Get Down?

How do rock climbers get down? Many routes can be rappelled (ruh-PELD). When rock climbers rappel, they anchor the rope to the pitch. They use their harness to help them get back down from the rock. Rappelling climbers push out from the wall with their feet. They then slide down the rope until their feet meet the rock again. They keep doing this until they reach the ground.

Some rock climbers return to the base by simply climbing back down. This is called downclimbing. Other times there is a path or road that leads down from the pitch.

This person is rappelling back down from the pitch. Rappelling can be the fastest, safest way back down.

The Great Indoors?

Have you ever been to a sporting goods store that had a rock-climbing wall? These walls are often used for shoppers to try out the store's goods. There are also many indoor rock-climbing courses.

Indoor rock climbing can be a safe way to learn and to practice the skills and maneuvers needed to climb real rock walls. Most indoor rock-climbing walls are not as tall as outdoor routes. There is little danger of falling. Indoor rock climbing is an excellent way to practice finding holds in the rock.

Most rock-climbing centers have walls that are safe for young people to climb. This young climber finds holds for his hands and feet.

Danger!

The biggest danger of rock climbing is falling. Falls can be deadly. For this reason, rock climbers should never climb alone. Climbers can work together to save each other. If one climber falls, the other climber can lock the rope and stop the fall. This is called arresting the fall.

Falling climbers could hit the rock wall. This is why climbers should always wear a helmet. A helmet also keeps climbers from getting hurt by falling rocks and even falling climbing equipment.

Both these climbers wear a helmet and take their time as they climb. They are working together to make sure they finish the climb safely.

Safe Climbing

Rock climbing can be dangerous, but good rock climbers are always careful. Most rock climbers practice for years before they make hard climbs.

All that practice helps keep people safe when they climb. Most rock-climbing leaders have lots of skill and knowledge. Rock climbing is a lot safer than it used to be, too. People have gotten better at it over the years. Climbers know more skills and maneuvers than the old mountaineers did. They also have better ropes and equipment. In fact, making and selling rock-climbing equipment is a big business. Thousands of people climb safely every year.

Climbers count on their equipment to keep them safe. They make sure everything, from harnesses to cams, is in good shape before climbing.

Living on the Edge

Rock climbing lets people test themselves in a way they could not do in any other sport. Rock climbing also offers beautiful views that can only be seen by climbing.

If you think you might want to try rock climbing someday, there are some things you can do to get ready. You can go to an indoor climbing course to learn how to find holds for your hands and feet. You can find a rock-climbing teacher to teach you how to climb and to use the equipment. Maybe you will find that this is the sport for you!

GLOSSARY

anchors (AN-kerz) Objects that hold something in place, usually fixed to a rope.

carabiners (ker-uh-BEE-nerz) Rings that hold and lock rope.

dangerous (DAYN-jeh-rus) Might cause hurt.

equipment (uh-KWIP-mint) All the supplies needed to do something.

explorer (ek-SPLOR-er) A person who travels and looks for new land.

extreme sport (ek-STREEM SPORT) A bold and uncommon sport, such as skateboarding, BMX, and wakeboarding.

harness (HAR-nes) The ties, bands, and other pieces that hold something or someone in place.

hooks (HUKS) Objects that curl in at one end.

maneuvers (muh-NOO-verz) Moves.

thrill (THRIL) A feeling of pleasure.

INDEX

B
belayer, 13

C
cams, 9
carabiners, 9

E
England, 7

G
Germany, 7

H
harness(es), 9, 15
helmet, 19
hold(s), 13, 22

I
Italy, 7

P
pitch, 13, 15

R
rock-climbing
    wall(s), 17

Y
Yosemite Decimal
    System, 11

WEB SITES

Due to the changing nature of Internet links, PowerKids Press has developed an online list of Web sites related to the subject of this book. This site is updated regularly. Please use this link to access the list:
www.powerkidslinks.com/edge/climb/